The Romance of Wine

Ben Gale

And wine that maketh glad the heart of man.

Psalms 104:15

JERUSALEM ◆ NEW YORK

About The Author

Ben Gale seems to have been born a Zionist. One day his beloved teacher, Mar Cheshin, returned to his native Jerusalem from New York. Ben would have followed him anywhere - and he did! He stowed away on the same boat, in 1929, only to be returned to the port in Boston after being discovered by the Captain.

In World War II he flew in a U.S. B25 bomber. At one time, while grounded in a sand storm in the Negev, he made his way to Tel Aviv. War time Tel Aviv, with its little blackout purple lights and smell of jasmine and orange blossoms in the air, made the author a bit heady. He went from one night club to another, cut in and danced with a lovely girl named Zilla who became his wife - this year celebrating their 50th wedding anniversary!

After the war, he returned to Israel under the G.I. Bill of Rights and pioneered the building of fish ponds. Upon his return to California, he went to work for the Sebastiani family winery where he learned all about and promoted wine with great zeal. He retired from the winery with honors and returned to Israel, where the seeds for
THE ROMANCE OF WINE
were gathered.

The author gorging himself with clusters of grapes in a Sicilian vineyard after the invasion of Sicily in 1943.

Acknowledgments

Cheshin Street in Jerusalem

Many thanks to Sir Martin Gilbert - historian, official biographer of Winston Churchill - for reading my script and finding it fascinating. His friendship is greatly appreciated.

I am indebted to the late Supreme Court Judge, Shneor Cheshin, my inspiring teacher and magnetic personality, who taught me Hebrew and led me through the pathways of the Bible and to Eretz Yisrael. I was a stowaway on a boat to get there.

To the Sebastiani family winery of Sonoma Valley, California, where I learned a great deal about wine.

To Zilla, my sabra wife, whose help was indispensable.

One night, very late, I get a call from Murray Greenfield - I just finished reading The Romance of Wine and it's fun reading!
Thanks to Murray, Ilan and Dror of Gefen Publishing House.

Introduction

The Romance of wine and the Bible go hand in hand ever since Noah left the ark and planted a vineyard.

Wine is bottled poetry, said Robert Louis Stevenson on his honeymoon in the wine country of northern California. And Beethoven proclaimed: I am the Bacchus who presses out the glorious wine for mankind.

King Solomon in his Song of Songs declares: Thy love is better than wine… let us get up early to the vineyards… let us see whether the vine blossoms and the pomegranates be in flower… there will I give thee my love.

The ancient Greek poet Euripides thought there could be no love without wine.

A rare mention of wine in whiskey country by a famous Western writer: Her gaze like wine had an exhilirating effect.

Riders of the Purple Sage
Zane Grey

A book of verses underneath the bough,
A jug of wine, a loaf of bread,
And thou beside me
Singing in the Wilderness.

Omar Khayyam

Oh, oh, kisses sweeter than wine...

On the Banjo, hit song of 1951
Pete Seeger

The Gift of Wine

The sun with all those planets revolving around it and dependent on it, can still ripen a bunch of grapes as if it had nothing else in the universe to do.

Galileo

Nothing more excellent or valuable than wine was ever granted by the gods to man.

Plato

Never think of leaving wines to your heir. Administer these yourself and let him have the money.

The Roman poet Martial

6000 years ago a Persian farmer squeezed a handful of ripe grapes into a gourd. When he came back a few days later to drink the juice, nature had given him wine!

Magic in your Glass
Wine Institute, California

Wine is mentioned more than 200 times in the Bible.

> Story of Wine
> Wine Institute, California

Wine was first mentioned in the Bible when Noah became a tiller of the soil and planted a vineyard and became the first winegrower!

> Genesis 9:20-22

There are few better gifts than wine.

> In his book David (King of Israel)
> Duff Cooper

Thanksgiving

...after you have gathered in from your threshing floor and your winepress, you shall rejoice in your feast.

> Deuteronomy 16:13-14

So shall thy barns be filled with plenty.
Any thy vats shall overflow with new wine.

> Proverbs 3:10

And wine that maketh glad the heart of man.

> Psalms 104:15

Offer unto God thanksgiving.

> Psalms 50:14, 107:22

For the harvest is ripe, come tread ye;
For the winepress is full - the vats overflow...

> Joel 4:13

Grape harvests in Biblical times were celebrated with joy. Farmers and their families gathered for singing and dancing and cutting the ripened grapes which were brought in baskets to the winepress. Grapes were tread by foot and the juice run off into a lower vat. Nature then took over and turned the juice into wine. The new wine was sealed in jars and stored in cool rock cellars.

Hundreds of winepresses were discovered throughout Israel. At Neot Kedumim, one with a large beautiful mosaic floor is quite impressive.

The country was blessed with wine. Jacob's blessing to his son Judah: His eyes shall be red with wine and his teeth white with milk... his royal garments of red would be washed in wine, in the blood of grapes.

Genesis 49:12,11

Pruning

Pruning one's vineyard comes in for special mention in the Bible:

For six years you may prune your vineyard, but in the seventh year the land shall rest… (lie fallow).

Leviticus 25:3-4

I am the true vine, and my Father is the vine dresser. Every branch of mine that bears no fruit he takes away, and every branch that does bear fruit he prunes that it may bear more fruit.

John 15:1-2

Ancient Jewish coin, grape leaf with vine branch and tendril. Reverse side - amphora or wine jug with inscription "Deliverance of Zion" struck during the first revolt of the Jews against the Romans 66-70 CE.

The first coin of the state of Israel (1949)

Isaiah had a vision of a world without war (2:4):

And they shall beat their swords into plowshares, And their spears into pruning-hooks.

Nation shall not lift up sword against nation, Neither shall they learn war any more.

A fascinating Biblical find is the Gezer Calendar - about 950 BCE. The tablet was written in ancient Hebrew, and is perhaps the first Farmer's Almanac. It lists the farm chores for the year, which include two months of pruning.

Skirball Museum, Hebrew Union College

Well Being

I can do no better than to state these words from the Talmud, Brachot 35b: Wine nourishes, refreshes and cheers. Wine is the foremost of all medicines; wherever wine is lacking, medicine becomes necessary.

> Wine and Your Well-Being
> Dr. Salvatore Lucia

Wine is the most healthful and hygienic drink there is.

> Louis Pasteur

𝑆ays Dr. S. Lucia: Wine is a natural tranquilizer, euphoric and soporific. Galen, the ancient Greek physician called wine the nurse of old age.

𝐴 60 Minutes reporter displaying a bottle of red wine on T.V. reported that Frenchmen, who eat a richer diet than Americans, have less heart disease because they wash down the rich food with lots of red wine!

𝑀ountain air as pure as wine.

Jerusalem of Gold
Naomi Shemer

Arrival of Spring

For lo, the winter is past,
The rains are over and gone;
The flowers appear on the earth.
The time of the singing of the birds has come,
And the voice of the turtledove is heard in our land;
The fig tree puts forth its green figs,
And the vines with the tender grapes
Give forth their fragrance.

Song of Songs 2:11-13

When Solomon aged, his outlook on life changed. Disillusionment and the futility of it all took hold and it reflected in Ecclesiastes: Vanity of vanities… all is vanity… what does man profit by all his labor? (1:2-3)… a time to be born and a time to die (3:2)… there is nothing new under the sun. (1:9)

Yet Solomon tells us to enjoy life!
I searched in my heart how to pamper my flesh with wine. (2:3)

Eat thy bread with joy and drink thy wine with a merry heart. (9:7)

A feast is made for laughter and wine maketh life happy. (10:19)

Wine is constant proof that God loves us and loves to see us happy.

Benjamin Franklin

O vine, come thou and reign over us!
And the vine said to the trees: Should I leave my wine
which cheereth God and man…?

Judges 9:12-13

Solomon spoke 3000 proverbs and his songs were a thousand and five. He was the author of Proverbs, Ecclesiastes and the Song of Songs.

I Kings 5:12

The wisdom of the wise and the experience of the ages are perpetuated by quotations.

Benjamin Disraeli

A Favorable Report

For the Lord your God is bringing you into a good land, a land of brooks and water, flowing forth in valleys and hills, a land of wheat and barley, of grapevines and fig trees and pomegranates, a land of olive trees and honey.

Deuteronomy 8:7

The above are the oft-mentioned Seven Species in the Bible. However, the most important agricultural crops of ancient Israel were wheat, barley, wine and olive oil.

Moses sent spies to spy out Canaan, the Promised Land. Joshua and Caleb brought back a favorable report that it was a land that floweth with milk and honey. It was harvest time in Canaan and they returned with figs and pomegranates and a cluster of grapes so large that it took two men to carry it on a pole.

Numbers 13:23

Again shalt thou plant vineyards upon the mountains of Samaria.

Jeremiah 31:5

Josephus Flavius, in the Wars of the Jews and Romans, records a cluster of grapes as tall as a man.

Jewish Symbols in the Greco-Roman Period
Edwin R. Goodenough

From the same source - Josephus describes the vine as magnificently represented in Herod's Temple as a symbol. Symbols of wine appeared on Jewish graves, tombs, wine jars, coins etc. The vine was represented more often than any other symbol.

The scene of two men carrying a giant cluster of grapes on a pole is the logo of the Israel Ministry of Tourism and Carmel Wines.

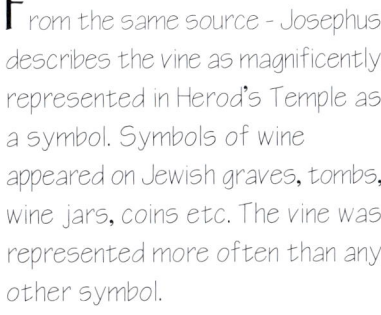

When the Crusaders in the Holy Land returned to Europe, they took back with them many choice vines which were planted in France. In the 1880s Baron Edmund de Rothschild of France brought back to the Holy Land many of the same varieties of choice vines. This was the start of the modern wine industry in Israel.

Benjamin Disraeli: A people that celebrate the wine harvest even when it does not reap grapes any more, will regain its vineyards.

Whose Jerusalem ?
Eliyahu Tal

Hospitality

They shall plant vineyards and drink the wine thereof.

Amos 9:14

She is a woman of valor... she makes plans for a vineyard and buys it, and with the fruit of her hands she planted a vineyard.

Proverbs 31:10-16

She hath set up her home with wisdom... she offers her hospitality: Come eat of my bread and drink of the wine that I have mingled.

Proverbs 9:1,5

Thy wife shall be as a fruitful vine by the sides of thy house; thy children like olive plants round about thy table.

Psalms 128:3

Melchizedek, king of Salem (Jerusalem), brought bread and wine to Abraham. The king's hospitality was a tribute to Abraham's bravery when he and his men defeated the hostile forces that had taken his nephew Lot captive.

Genesis 14:14-18

When you come into your neighbor's vineyard and eat grapes-as much as you enjoy eating, do not put any into a vessel to carry away.

Deuteronomy 23:25

Holiday of Love

It is a unique and romantic holiday celebrated only in Israel.

It arrives on the 15th of the Hebrew month of Av (Tu B'Av) - always under a full moon according to the Hebrew lunar calendar. The origin of the holiday stems from the Bible:

And they commanded the children of Benjamin saying: Go and lie in wait in the vineyards, and see and behold if the daughters of Shiloh come out to dance, and catch you every man his wife and go to the land of Benjamin!

Judges 21:20-21

Invitation to a moonlight hike celebrating the Holiday of Love near Masada

Rabbi Simon Ben Gamliel said: There are no happier days for Israel than the 15th of Av and the Day of Atonement, for on them the daughters of Jerusalem would go forth to dance in the vineyards. What did they say?
Young man lift your eyes and see what you would choose for yourself.

Mishna, Ta'anit 4:8

The 608th Commandment

הילולים

VIN NOUVEAU DRY WHITE WINE בכורי יין לבן יבש

Maimonides compiled a list of 613 commandments from the Five Books of Moses, called the Taryag Mitzvot.

Of particular interest is the 608th commandment which deals with the military. If a man takes a wife, builds a house, plants a vineyard - he should be deferred from (military) service for one year.

How important it was to provide a home and vineyard! The prophet Micah (4:4): Every man under his vine and under his fig tree...

And they shall build houses, and inhabit them; And they shall plant vineyards, and eat the fruit of them.

> Isaiah 65:21

Let me sing of my well-beloved...
My well-beloved had a vineyard in a very fruitful hill;
And he digged it and cleared it of stones,
And planted it with the choicest vine,
And built a tower in the midst of it,
And also hewed out a winepress therein...

> Isaiah 5:1-2

The defense forces today may look with a little envy upon their Biblical brethren. However, even without a vineyard, no soldier need feel deprived of the fruit of the vine. There is always the friendly wine shop or bar or pub.
Samuel Johnson said back in 1777: There is nothing which has yet been contrived by which so much happiness is provided as by a good tavern or inn.

What though youth gave love and roses,
Age still leaves us friends and wine.

> Thomas Moore

Loose Lips

In vino veritas - the truth comes out in wine! The Talmud says: Wine got in and a secret got out.

The U.S. learned that lesson the hard way in World War II as a result of the bombing of Ploesti oil fields in Romania. After that disaster, it prominently displayed posters - LOOSE LIPS SINK SHIPS. Bomber crews trained for that mission in the North African desert near Benghazi. They frequented bars where the Nazis planted spies. Result - 60 planes lost!

Woe unto them that rise early in the morning and pursue strong drink, and tarry late into the night until wine inflame them.

> Isaiah 5:11

Woe unto him who makes his neighbor drunk.

> Habakkuk 2:15

There is evil in every berry of grape.

> The Koran

Come, come, good wine is a good familiar creature if it be well used; explain no more against it.

> Shakespeare

Ceremonies

Jesus apparently enjoyed wine but Matthew (11:19) looked askance upon it. In the New Testament, wine became a part of the religious ceremonial of the church.

With Israel's many ceremonies and festivities, the jug of wine was never too far away, but also near enough for everyday use.

The beginning of Sabbath is welcomed with wine - the Kiddush - and the end of Sabbath - the Havdalah, also with wine.

A boy is born and in the circumcision rite (Brit Milah) he gets his first taste of wine.

The bride lifts her veil at the wedding ceremony and shares a sip of wine with the groom.

The blessing over the fruit of the vine has its own separate blessing. No other drink enjoys that distinction.

Talmud, Brachot

The Scriptures abound with occasions for drinking wine. Just to mention two: Passover celebrates freedom from slavery and it is customary to drink four glasses of wine. But Purim - by the jugful! The beautiful and brave Queen Esther and her uncle Mordecai saved the Jews of Persia from annihilation. It is a joyous and fun holiday and it is customary to drink wine till one can't tell the difference (adloyada) between the good guy Mordecai and the bad guy Haman!

Coca Cola

There are taste harmonies between certain wines and certain foods. Just as mustard with hot-dogs, so red wine blends with red meat, pasta dishes and cheeses, and white wine with fish and fowl. White wine with their characteristic acidity, like pieces of lemon to overcome sea food fishy flavors are go-togethers. Taste preferences, however, are individual, and everyone drinks whatever wine he enjoys drinking.

Serving wine adds grace and makes for amicable conversation at the dinner table. It adds ceremony and tradition when guests toast each other with wine and clink glasses. Can you imagine doing this with Coca Cola?

> The Commonsense Book of Wine
> Leon D. Adams

Dining companions, regardless of gender, social standing, or the years they lived, should be chosen for their ability to eat - and drink - with the right mixture of abandon and restraint. They should be able, no, eager, to sit for hours over a meal of soup and wine and cheese and other courses. Then with good friends of such attributes, and good food and good wine, we may well ask - when shall we live if not now?

Author unknown

Does one want to woo the ladies? Leon D. Adams writes about a man called Lucien Johnson who is the acknowledged expert on the subject. Says Lucien: The wine with which to woo a lady is not champagne. Champagne only makes folks talkative. But Burgundy, (full-bodied red dry wine) warmed to the temperature of the room, makes people affectionate.
Yes, Burgundy is the only love wine!

Moderation

Give strong drink unto him that is ready to perish, and wine unto the bitter in soul. Let him drink and forget his poverty and remember his misery no more.

Proverbs 31:6-7

Greek Krater for mixing wine and water

Give me a bowl of wine - in this I bury all unkindness.

Shakespeare

A woman drove me to drink and I never even had the courtesy to thank her.

W.C. Fields

Wine makes a person more pleased with himself; I do not say it makes him more pleasing to others.

Samuel Johnson

I drink to make other people interesting.

George Jean Nathan

Drink moderately, for drunkenness neither keeps a secret nor observes a promise.

Cervantes

Thomas Jefferson, the author of the American Declaration of Independence, advocated wine as a beverage of temperance.
If you can't drink in moderation, then don't drive and leave your horse and buggy at home! After all, what are friends for?

Men who can have communion in nothing else... can still rise into some glow of brotherhood over food and wine.

Thomas Carlyle

From wine what sudden friendship springs.

John Gay

Wine helps people socially and in fellowship. Sipping wine is fine when it brings people together who are distant from one another.

Mishna, Sanhedrin 104

Ruth and Boaz

And when ye reap the harvest of your land, thou shall not reap the corner of thy field, neither shalt thou gather the gleaning of thy harvest. And thou shalt not glean thy vineyard; neither shalt thou gather the fallen grapes of thy vineyard. Thou shalt leave them for the poor and for the stranger.

Leviticus 19:9-10

Ruth of Moab, a widow, would not leave her Israelite mother-in-law Naomi: Wither thou goest, I will go, and where thou lodgest, I will lodge. Thy people shall be my people and thy God my God.

Ruth 1:16

Ruth gleaned a field at harvest time that belonged to Boaz of Bethlehem. They met. They ate. He said to her: Come hither and eat of the bread and dip thy morsel in the vinegar.

Ruth 2:14

Fragment of a wine jug found at Masada in a garbage dump, about 2000 years old. Inscription reads: "Herod, King of the Jews."

If grape-gatherers came to thee, would they not leave some gleaning grapes?

Obadiah 1:5

The rest is romance and history. Ruth the Moabitess became the great-grandmother of King David!

Ruth 4:21-22

The Survivor

The story of Ruth's ancestor Moab is the story of the birth of a nation born out of incest. Moab was conceived in a cave with the aid of a jug of wine!

Lot, his wife and two daughters were fleeing from Sodom and Gomorrah when those cities of sin were being destroyed by fire and brimstone. Lot's wife looked back and turned into a pillar of salt!

The two daughters of Lot, fearing that they and their father were the only survivors in the world, decided on having children to carry on.

With a jug of wine - they got their father drunk and took turns in a cave sleeping with him. Thus were born Moab and Ammon who in later years became fathers of nations - and left their mark in Bible history!

Genesis 19

Freedom from Fear

Every man under his vine and under his fig tree and none shall make him afraid.

Micah 4:4

And they shall dwell safely and shall build houses and plant vineyards.

Ezekiel 28:26

The wicked Queen Jezebel, wife of Ahab, King of Israel, had Navot, the owner of a vineyard, stoned to death on a false charge. The king then took possession. The prophet Elijah was outraged at this miscarriage of justice. He said to Ahab: Hast thou killed and also taken possession? He told Ahab he would die and the dogs would lick his blood. Ahab died in battle. Jezebel was thrown to the dogs and the dogs ate her flesh!

1 Kings 21:1-23

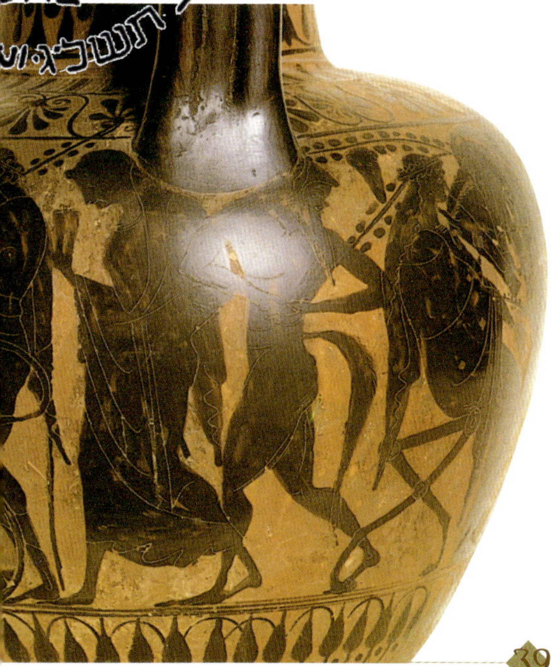

Roots

The House of Israel is the Vineyard of God.

Isaiah 5:7

Names of places: Beit Hakerem - meaning house of the vineyard; Kiryat Anavim - town of the grapes; Carmel - vineyard of God; Kiryat Gat - town of the winepress.

Kerem Shalom - Vineyard of Peace

Israelis are moving fast forward - back to their roots! They are taking names like Carmi, meaning my vineyard, and Gefen, meaning vine and many other Hebrew names. The family name of former prime minister Levi Eshkol means "a cluster of grapes."

The prophet Ezekiel (chapter 27) gives a fascinating account of trading ships and the trade in "wine of Helbon." Illustrated above is a Jewish merchant ship of the third century CE. It was reconstructed according to an engraving in a burial cave in Beit Shearim.

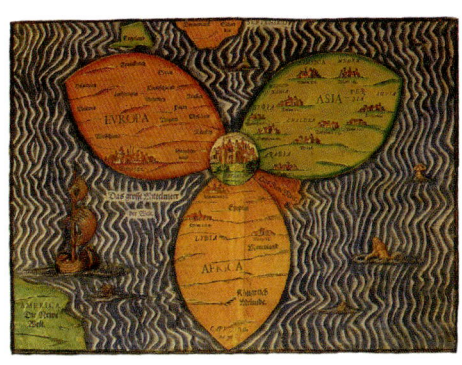

Jerusalem, center of the world, map by Heinrich Bunting, 1585

Clay Jars

Clay jars, also called amphora, were used in the fermentation of wine and for storage. They had pointed bases which were stuck in the ground to hold them upright. The pointed bases were also convenient for shipping wine. They fit into the slanted hull bottom of a vessel.

Clay wine jars were recovered from an ancient sunken vessel off the coast of Israel, now in the museum at Dor. A hole appears in the shoulder of the jar to allow for the escape of gas when fermentation takes place.

A royal storage jar displayed at the Israel Museum has a seal on handle - Conconai Lamelech - meaning jars belonging to the king. Superior wines were inscribed <u>Soog A</u> - meaning <u>Grade A'</u>, and <u>Moovchar</u> - meaning choice wine - and place of origin like Motza.

The last word on jars: It's not the jar that matters but the good old wine that's in it!

                Sayings of the Fathers 4:27

Cupbearer

Joseph and Pharaoh's chief cupbearer were jail mates. Joseph interpreted the latter's dream and the disturbing dreams of Pharaoh who then made Joseph the ruler of Egypt.

Genesis 41

And when the Queen of Sheba had seen all the wisdom of Solomon, and the house that he had built… and his cupbearers… there was no more spirit in her.

I Kings 10:4-5

"The Splendour of Persia" is splendidly displayed at the Bible Lands Museum, Jerusalem. Stelae (carved in stone) show servants carrying wine to the king. One with a wineskin slung over his shoulder and another bearing a chalice with a lid. Rare vintages were carried in small bowls.

The lavishness of the palace wine festivities is described in the Book of Esther.

A cupbearer to the king was often rewarded with a high position. Nehemia was cupbearer to the Persian king. He pleaded with the king to allow him to go to Judah to rebuild its walls which lay in ruins. The king granted his wish. Nehemia became governor of Judah.

Nehemia 1:1-4, 5:14

English - Hebrew Glossary

The following Hebrew words are transliterated. Pronounce the CH as in Bach, the German composer, and the G as in "go." Pronounce the A like in Arthur. (A few exceptions.)

aging: hit-yash-noot
Young red wines are often harsh. Aging can give wine a desirable aroma and bouquet. White wines are consumed young when they are fresh and fruity.

alcohol: co-hel
The result of fermentation of grape juice.

balanced wine: ya-yin meh-ooh-zan
A wine possessing the right proportion of grape sugar and acidity and other principal constituents.

blend: ta-a-rovet
Blending is the art of mixing wines of various qualities and characteristics to make a rounded wine and achieve uniformity from year to year.

consumer: ha-tsarkan

dry wine: ya-yin yavesh
The opposite of sweet; free of sugar.

enology: torat ha-ya-yin
The science of wine making. Usually a graduate enologist is responsible for the wine making procedure of a winery.

fermentation: tsee-sa
The chemical action of yeast on grape sugar which transforms the sugar into equal parts of carbon dioxide (it bubbles away) and alcohol.

fragrance: nee-cho-ach

grape harvest: ba-tseer

grapes: a-na-vim

nouveau: nuvo
A wine ready to drink after harvest and fresh from the vat. It is an old French tradition that Frenchmen eagerly look forward to November 15 when nouveau makes its appearance in the cafes of Paris and elsewhere.

red wine: ya-yin a-dom
Gets its color from the grape skins.

restaurant: mis-a-da

rosé wine: ya-yin rozay

semi-dry (semi-sweet): cha-tsee yavesh

smell: ray-ach
"What gives pleasure to the soul rather than to the body? Smell!" (Brachot 43b)

sweet wine: ya-yin matok

table wine: ya-yin shul-chanee

taste, flavor: ta-am
Ssniff the aroma and bouquet. Aroma is the fragrance of the wine that originates from the grape. Bouquet is the more subtle fragrance that comes from fermenting and aging.

thanksgiving: ho-da-ya

varietal wine: ya-yin zanee
In Israel, a wine containing at least 85% of the grape appearing on the label. Examples - Cabernet Sauvignon and Sauvignon Blanc.

vin ordinaire, ordinary wine: ya-yin ra-geel
French term meaning good, sound, inexpensive.

vine: gefen

vineyard: kerem

vintage: onat ba-tseer

vintner: yay-nan
A producer of wine. A wine merchant.

white wine: ya-yin lavan

wine: ya-yin
The fermented juice of fresh ripe grapes. Wine is a product of nature. Nature covers the grapes on the vine with a dust-like bloom which is a wild yeast. When the grapes are crushed and the juice released, the yeast "eats" the natural sugar in the juice. That causes a fermentation and turns the juice into wine.

winegrower, winemaker: korem

winery: yekev

yeast: shma-rim
"Next to the grape, yeast is the most important element of wine, for the microscopic plant organism is the sole producer of fermentation that changes grape juice into wine... Wild yeast is less than predictable. Hence, cultural yeast strains are in widespread use in today's winemaking."
 - Sam Sebastiani

Copyright © Gefen Publishing House Ltd.
Jerusalem 1999/5759

All rights reserved. No part of this publication may be translated, reproduced, stored in a retrieval system or transmitted, in any form or by any means, electronic, mechanical, photocopying, recording or otherwise, without express written permission from the copyright owner and the publisher.

Design:	Studio Rami & Jaki, Jerusalem
Photo credits:	Yochanan Ben Yaacov,
	Oded Feingarsh, Rimona Gale

Edition 9 8 7 6 5 4 3 2 1

Gefen Publishing House Ltd.
POB 36004, Jerusalem 91360, Israel
isragefen@netmedia.net.il
972-2-538-0247

Gefen Books
12 New St., Hewlett, NY 11557, USA
gefenbooks@compuserve.com
1-800-477-5257

Printed in Israel
Send for our free catalogue

Library of Congress Cataloging-in-Publication Data
Gale, Ben, 1914-
    The romance of wine / Ben Gale.

ISBN 965 229 172 2

    1. Wine and wine making. I. Title.
    TP548.G177   1999
641.2'2--dc21   97-19651
                                                   CIP